OPTIONS TRADING FOR BEGINNERS

THE GUIDE FOR MAKING MONEY WITH OPTIONS TRADING

state and local laws governing professional licensing, business practices, advertising and all other aspects of doing business in the US, Canada, UK or any other jurisdiction is the sole responsibility of the purchaser or reader.

Neither the author nor the publisher assumes any responsibility or liability whatsoever on the behalf of the purchaser or reader of these materials. Any perceived slight of any individual or organization is purely unintentional.

Table of Contents

INTRODUCTION

I want to thank you and commend you for reading the book, "Options Trading for Beginners".

How would you like to leverage your portfolio and make very nice extra profits? People trading options do it every day, and you can, too. This book will introduce you to the concepts behind options, introduce the vocabulary associated with options trading and give you some online resources for further education and for actually trading options. If you take advantage of the information herein and follow up with more education and training on the topic of options trading, you will be in a position to earn bigger profits in the stock market by trading options. The better you get at trading options, the more money you can make. We also point out that options trading is not risk-free. There are certain fundamentals that must be followed and the trader must keep abreast of the stock market and the options market in order to minimize the risk. Make no mistake; options trading is not for the faint of heart. There is some level of stress and risk involved and the trader must commit to spending the time and energy to learn the business and operate with a satisfactory level of comfort and confidence to be successful.

This book also assumes the reader has a good familiarity with the stock market. We cannot include all of the nuances of the market in the financial instruments underlying the trading in options. We have attempted to offer an introduction to options trading and how to do so successfully. To make the examples more realistic, we usually use real stocks and market information at the time of writing this book. Trading in options is not all that difficult, but you do have to pay attention, learn the concepts and the vocabulary, and understand the basics of options trading. We wish you good fortune in carrying out options trading and making the kind of profits you desire.

CHAPTER 1 CONCEPTS BEHIND OPTIONS

A. Options are Derivatives

Financial instruments are a varied lot and are changing and growing all the time, sometimes rapidly. Everyone has heard about derivatives. Derivatives are simply financial instruments whose value depends on the value of some other instrument. The financial instruments commonly referred to are things like stocks, municipal bonds, notes, commercial bonds, ETF's, index funds, and so many more. Options are just another financial instrument, but they are a form of a derivative. That is, the value of the option depends on the value of the underlying financial instrument.

An option is a choice because you have the option to act on the contract or not, depending on your decisions and the market conditions. Normally, we would act on an option if the decision is in our favor and not if it is to our disadvantage. That is a strong argument for dealing in options. However, in most cases, you are not required to act on the contract, an action called execution of the option. You don't have to if you don't want to. On the other hand, if you buy an option to buy at the contract terms, the seller of that contract is required to sell under those terms. That part of options is a one-way street. Historically, only 10% of options are exercised, that is acted upon, 60% are traded before expiration and the remaining 30% expire worthless.

B. Trading in Options Has Both Risks and Rewards

Trading in options is not without risk, especially for new traders. It is remarkably easy to lose money trading in options. All it takes is a few bad decisions, which are frequently based on lack of understanding on the part of the investor or by not paying attention. We strongly recommend trading only with risk capital. That is, money you can afford to lose if things go bad. Don't trade in options with the rent money or the money set aside for the kid's college education.

This book is designed to help you avoid those mistakes by providing an introductory understanding. Can you trade in options without reading or studying the subject? Of course, but no one can speak a new language without first studying it. Same thing with options trading. This book will get you started by pointing out the fundamentals, but you, the investor, must continue to study and learn, hopefully before you start trading options. Importantly, some of the resources listed in Chapter 7 offer virtual trading platforms, in which you can trade with virtual money, not your own. This is free training and allows you to learn without losing real money. Besides, it is fun.

C. Pick Your Own Trading Strategy

Your trading strategy can be **speculative, income, or conservative**. A **speculative** strategy is based on predicting the timing and amount of any movement in the price of the stock. A **conservative** strategy involves trading in a manner that protects against large losses for equities the investor owns. An **income** strategy is one under which you generate regular income above that from normal stock gains or dividends. We will cover these in due course.

Usually, options are based on common stocks. We will follow that custom, but options are available for many different instruments like ETF's and Stock Indices. It's just easier to understand with stocks.

D. Option Trading Uses its Own Vocabulary

When you understand a few basic concepts and some vocabulary, you will see that it is not all that complicated. However, you have to study not only the market, but the ins and outs of options trading, too. Now, some of the vocabulary may seem arcane, but it is the "lingo" of Wall Street and is used by all traders and brokers everywhere. You will need to understand this vocabulary to understand the business of options trading.

E. Decide to Pay Attention

Remember, if you choose to trade in options, you have new opportunities but also new responsibilities. If you are holding options on a stock or other instrument, you must keep a close eye on it. There is nothing automatic about options. If you hold an option and it suddenly becomes very valuable, it is up to you to act on it. It will not act on its own, in fact, it may expire and you will lose the premium cost and any value of the option.

Under some circumstances, you may be assigned, which means you are required to act on the option. Apart from assignments, nobody is going to call you and ask you what you want to do. You have to follow it closely, but that is interesting and sometimes, exciting.

We assume in this book that you are already familiar with trading in the stock market but somewhat new to trading in options. We can't teach you all the fundamentals of stock market trading and options trading in one book, but we can give you a peek at trading in options. We do, however, offer some information about the stock market in the context of trading in options.

Chapter 2 Basic Vocabulary for Options

Whenever you explore a new topic; mathematics, chemistry, or astronomy, for example, you have to first understand the vocabulary. For instance, the word integrate means one thing in Calculus and something totally different in Social Science. We will start with some definitions and add more vocabulary as we go along. We will identify new vocabulary with a pointer symbol like this ►. Please don't get discouraged at the large vocabulary. Most of it makes sense and the new options investor will learn the vocabulary as she makes more and more trades. It will begin to come naturally and soon you will sound like an expert.

► **Option**: an option is a contract that allows you to buy or sell a particular financial instrument at a specified amount on or before some contract expiration date. For equity stocks, the option contract is based on 100 shares. The due date or expiration date is the closing of the market on the third Friday of the month of the contract. For example, if you buy an August option for 2016, it will expire on August 19, the third Friday of August, 2016.

▶ **Put Option:** a put option is an option contract to **sell** a particular stock under the terms of the put option contract. With a put option, you are 'putting it into the ownership' of the option buyer.

▶ **Call Option**: a call option is a contract to **buy** a stock according to the terms of the call option contract. A call option means you are calling upon the seller to sell you the stock, at the contract terms.

▶ **Long and Short:** Call options have two subsets; long and short. When you buy a call option to open a trade, you are said to be buying a long call. When you sell a call option to close a trade, you are selling a long call. When you sell a call to open a trade, you are said to be selling a short call. When you act to close that trade, you are buying a short call. As the price of the stock rises, your call option also rises in value.

▶ **Writer**: a writer is an investor who sells an option, like a call or a put.

►**Holder**: a holder is someone who buys an option, i.e., holds the option.

► **Bid Price**: a writer buys at the bid price, and the holder sells at the bid price. Think of the writer as 'bidding' to buy the option at the bid price.

► **Ask Price**: a writer sells at the ask price and a holder buys at the ask price. Think of the writer 'asking' the ask price to sell an option.

► **American Option**: an American option is an option, whether a put or a call, that can be exercised at any time before the expiration date. American options are usually sold on the stock market.

► **European Option**: a European option can only be exercised on the expiration date, not before. However, it can be sold prior to the expiration date. European options are generally sold on the "Over The Counter" or OTC market.

► **Buyer and Seller**: for every purchase or sale there must be a sale or purchase that corresponds with it. The table below describes that correspondence for the buyer and seller.

Notice that the buyer has the option but not the obligation to act, whereas the seller has the obligation to act if the buyer chooses to execute the option. Here, we refer in the most general sense to an investment 'instrument' which could be a common stock or, for example, an ETF.

	Buyer	Seller
Call Option	Right to buy the particular instrument	Obligation to sell the particular instrument
Put Option	Right to sell the particular instrument	Obligation to buy the particular instrument

► **Execute**: this means that the buyer decides to act on the contract, to buy or sell; that is to execute the contract. It is also referred to as Exercising the Option.

► **Expiration Date**: when the contract is agreed upon, it runs for some finite period of time. After the expiration date, the contract expires; that is it is no longer valid. After the expiration date, the value of the option is zero.

► **Strike Price**: the strike price is the stock price agreed to in the put or call option contract. For example, if you were to buy a call contract for Google (GOOG) at $695, that means you have the right but not the obligation to buy 100 shares of Google stock at $695. That is the strike price. It is also called the Exercise Price. Similarly, a put option for GOOG will have its own strike price.

▶ **Assignment**: to be assigned means that an option you hold has experienced some event which requires you to respond. Reaching the expiration date with a stock put option that is in the money requires you to deliver the stock.

▶ **Market Price**: market price is the current price of that stock today. Market prices vary minute by minute on the stock exchange.

▶ **Option Premium**: there is a cost for buying an options contract, either put or call. That charge, collected by the seller, depends on the length of the contract and the practice of the broker. Premiums can range from a few cents per contract to closer to $20. Option premiums are paid in cash, the cash you have in your brokerage account.

▶ **Intrinsic Value**: Value of the premium derived from the value of the underlying stock.

▶ **Extrinsic Value**: Portion of the premium related to volatility and time.

▶ **Commission**: a buyer of an option has to pay the broker to carry out that purchase or sale, just as she has to pay a commission for the sale or purchase of any stock or other instrument.

▶ **At, In and Out of the Money**: when you own call options on a particular stock, if the market price is the same as the strike price, you are said to be 'at the money.' If you buy a call option and the market price is above the strike price, you are 'in the money.' Similarly, again for a call option, if the market price is below the strike price, you are 'out of the money.' You would have no profit motivation to exercise the option when you are out of the money, for either a put or call option. These are often abbreviated as ATM, ITM and OTM.

Example

To illustrate, if you buy an option for General Motors (GM) with a strike price of $29.00 and GM is selling at $29, you are **'at the money**.' With that same option, if GM is trading at $25, you are, at your option, able to buy GM for $29 but since it is trading at $25, you would lose money doing so. You are **'out of the money'**, literally, by $4 per share or $400, because the contract covers 100 shares. Not a smart move. Add to that loss the premium and commission costs and you lose even more.

On the other hand, if GM is trading at $34 you are **'in the money'** if you hold a call option for 100 shares of GM at $29 when the market is at $34. Nice move. Of course you still have to pay the premium which might have been say, $3.00 so your profit is $3,400-$2,900 - $300 or a net gain of $200. Subtract the commission and you have a profit. Not bad for one trade.

This table will help you understand At, In, and Out of the money positions. It is based on the example above, GM with a strike price of $29. The premium and commission costs are not included. As you know, commissions are usually a fixed fee, regardless of the value of the trade. The premium will depend on the value of the underlying stock and the time left before expiration.

GM at $29.00 Strike Price

Market Price	Call Option	Put Option	Call Gain/Loss	Put Gain/Loss
25.00	Out of the Money	In the Money	4.00	4.00
27.00	Out of the Money	In the Money	2.00	2.00
29.00	At the Money	At the money	0	0
31.00	In the Money	Out of the Money	2.00	2.00
33.00	In the Money	Out of the Money	4.00	4.00

Notice that when the strike price and the market price are the same, both buyers of calls and sellers of puts are even. Nobody is ahead or behind. But when the market price moves, both puts and calls respond in value, either gain or loss.

Let's look at another example.

Suppose you have information that leads you to believe a particular stock will make a dramatic move in the near future. Maybe you have heard rumors that Lowes (LOW) is going to get a big contract that will take it to new levels. You check on it, as listed on the New York Stock exchange (NYSE) and find it is trading at about $78. But, you predict it will rise by some 10% to $86 but you don't have the cash to buy now or you choose not to buy now. You might buy a call option at $75 for which you will have to pay a premium of say,

$3.00, or $300 for the 100 share option. At that moment, you are out of the money (OTM). But, if you have predicted correctly, and it rises to say $87, you now have the opportunity to buy those 100 shares at $75, not $87. You are in the money on this contract (ITM) since the market price is above the strike price. If you want to hold stock in Lowes, you can exercise that option for $7500 + $300 (the premium) + commission, and hold 100 shares at $87 worth $8,700 but it only costs you $7,800, a neat profit of $900. In this case, the market price is $87 and the strike price is $75. Nice deal. Or, you could to buy the stock at $75 and immediately sell it at $87, making a profit of $900 for the 100 shares. On the other hand, if LOW drops in market price to say, $70, you are out of the money and would not want to exercise the call option. However, your loss of $300, the premium you paid for the option is much less than the $800 loss you would have incurred if you had bought LOW at market of $78 only to have it drop to $70.

Another example.

Maybe you have been watching a stock and you think it is going to drop in price for whatever reason. Maybe a new earnings report is coming out and the indications are that earnings are down. That is one of many reasons the price of a stock may drop. One recent example is Takata Corp. (TKTDY), the maker of automotive air bags. In early July, 2014, TKTDY was selling at about $40. As everyone knows now, they were about to suffer a massive recall of their product and the stock dropped severely. If you had owned TKTDY, you were about to take a huge loss. At that point, you could have bought a put option on TKTDY at say, a strike price of $40. This gives you the right to sell TKTDY for $40, regardless of the market price. If the stock had climbed in value, to say $50, you would be required to sell the stock you owned at $40, taking a loss. But, since you predicted correctly and the price plummeted, say to $9 as it did. Now, you can execute your put contract and sell at $40. This is a way to hedge your investment.

▶ **Hedge**: To hedge is to take an action that can protect an investment from serious losses under certain market conditions. It is like an insurance policy; in case something goes wrong, you can minimize downside losses.

▶ **Insider Trading**: Insider Trading is both tempting and illegal, in most countries. Insider Trading consists of making investment decisions based on information not available to the general public. If you act on information you read in the Wall Street Journal, that is not insider trading. If you act on information from your neighbor, who is a top level executive at the company, that is insider trading and is illegal.

▶ **Leverage**: Options trading gives you the chance to buy options for a whole lot less money than buying the underlying stock. Your dollar goes further trading options than by trading stocks and for a given amount of money you invest, you can control many more shares with options than you can with buying the stock itself.

▶ **Wasting Asset**: A wasting asset is one that declines in value over time. For options, the rate of decline becomes very rapid as the option approaches the expiration date. Of course, on the expiration date, the option's value goes to zero. This is the extrinsic value and is related to the time value of money.

▶ **LEAPS**: LEAPS is the acronym for Long-term Equity Anticipation Securities. LEAPS mostly behave just like all other options but instead of having a an expiration date of a few weeks or months, LEAPS have a lifetime of one or more years. This longer lifetime tends to smooth out the effects of volatility and allows, with the same leverage as regular options, the benefit of longer term performance of the underlying security. LEAPS are available for most commonly traded equity stocks and for equity indexes like the S&P 500.

▶ **Volatility**: Volatility in a stock is the characteristic variability of a stock's price on a day to day basis. Implied volatility is the expected change in market price of a stock in the near future. Volatility of a stock in the past is measured by Beta, a Greek letter we will discuss later in the chapter on Greeks, **Chapter 5, It's All Greek to Me.**

▶ **Open Interest:** this represents the total number of option contracts open at the time, whether they are puts or calls.

CHAPTER 3 TRADING OPTIONS, NOT STOCKS

Remember that a call option gives you the right to buy a stock at the strike price but not the obligation to do so. Using the previous example, maybe Lowes is not a stock you want to hold. It may not fit into your overall investment strategy, but at the time it goes over the strike price, the value of the option itself will increase. The value of the option will follow the market, up or down. Of course, since options are a wasting asset, their value declines over time and goes to zero at the expiration date.

However, someone else may be a big fan of LOW and wants to increase her holdings. She would love to buy LOW at $75, certainly more than she would be willing to buy at $87 so the call option would have value to her. You can sell the call option to her, transferring the opportunity to her, in exchange for a sales price. If the sales price or premium, which is based on the increase in value of the underlying stock is attractive, you can sell it and make a profit, without ever buying the LOW stock, itself. Slick.

Regarding LOW, on a recent day, LOW was selling at about $78 on the New York Stock Exchange. That same day, call options were selling for $5.90 to $0.09, depending upon the strike prices, that is whether they were ITM or OTM. Put options on that day were priced from $0.11 to $3.50, again depending on the strike price. These options were 3 days before expiration. Both put and call options that were in the money were the most valuable.

This points up the leverage of options. In this example, you could control 100 shares of LOW with a call option for an investment of anywhere from $9.00 to $590.00 rather than $7,800 for the 100 shares of the stock itself.

Example

On a particular day, Apple Inc. (AAPL) is selling for $95.91 on the NASDQ exchange. Alice, an investor, owns 100 shares of AAPL. She can buy a put option, called a covered put, with an expiration date some days from now, for $3.65 with a strike price of $99.50. She will collect $365 to do that but unless AAPL rises to above that price before the expiration date, she pockets the premium and keeps her stock in Apple Inc. Again, a smart investment without much risk, since the probability of AAPL moving that much within a few days is pretty low. However, if AAPL goes up to some price above $99.50, she will have to sell her stock at the strike price of $99.50, that is the contract will be assigned.

Chapter 4 Trading Strategies

One thing that should be obvious by now is that options trading is not a "set it and forget it" activity. You must be willing to watch the market itself and the options market also. Day trading is not for the faint of heart and options trading is like day trading in that options prices are always on the move. One can lose a lot of money or miss a lot of opportunities, by not paying attention. That does not mean you must be on your computer all the time, but it does mean you have to be fully engaged. We recommend that you look at your portfolio in terms of "long term holds," "short term holds" and "trading positions." We cannot recommend that you trade aggressively with the stocks you want for long term holds. Maybe you can experiment with some of your short term holds but it is more prudent to keep a separation between these sectors of your portfolio. In other words, don't bet farm with options. Instead, set aside some amount of Risk Capital, money you don't want to lose but money you can afford to lose if everything goes wrong.

▶ **Risk Capital**: money you can afford to put at risk. Money that, if you lose it, will not cause any significant damage to your financial position. This is not money set aside for the kids' college education or the rent money.

Different Strategies

We can define strategies as either speculative, conservative or income. Of course, no strategy is completely one or the other but if the investor plans well, the average risk/reward ratio can be anywhere in between. The level of risk versus reward can be imagined as a playground seesaw. As a general rule, the higher the risk in an investment, the higher the potential reward. But remember, there are no guarantees. Any investor who is young in age and has a good income from a stable job can afford more risk. At the other extreme, an older citizen, living on a fixed income cannot tolerate very much risk. For both types of investor, they may choose to adopt an income strategy which can result in regular income based on buying and selling a sequence of options on a particular schedule.

Every investor has to decide on an individual strategy that seeks to set a balance between risk and reward at the level suitable for themselves. There are several strategies that have different levels of risk and reward. Here are just a few examples:

	Bull Market	Bear Market	
Conservative	Buy Calls	Buy Puts	
	Buy Covered Calls	Sell Covered Calls	
	Buy Cash-Secured Puts	Bear Call Spread	
	Bull Put Spread	Bear Put Spread	
	Bull Call Spread		
Speculative	Buy Long Calls	Sell Naked Calls	
		Sell Covered Puts	
Income	Straddle	Straddle	
	Strangle	Strangle	

A. Buying Put and Call Options

When buying options, you have options. During the life of the option, that is from the day you buy it until it expires, you can sell it, exercise it or just let it expire.

Buying calls will profit you when a stock is expected to rise, for example in a bull market. For example, you may want to buy options on Microsoft Corporation, MSFT, which is trading now at $52. You could buy a call option with a strike price of $48.50 for $3.60 for a total investment of $310. Now, if MSFT increases in value, you can buy at the strike price. However, if the market price declines below $48.50, your option would be out of the money and you would choose to let the option expire and it would cost you the $360 premium.

On the other hand, if you forecast a strong drop in the price, i.e., a bear market, you can buy a put with a strike price of say, $50 for the amount of the premium. Now, if the market price drops below $50, say to $40 you can buy the stock at the lower market price and sell the same stock at the strike price of $50, and you pocket the gain of $10 per share, minus the premium. Or, you could sell the put and collect the premium. Then someone else can buy and sell the stock for a gain or loss.

B. Covered Calls

Covered calls is a strategy many investors will use when they start trading options. A covered call takes place when the investor owns a stock and decides to sell a call on that stock; i.e., the sale of the stock is covered by the stock owned by the investor. The main reason people do this is to gain additional earnings, for an out of the money stock. A covered call becomes profitable when it expires worthless, that is, it does not become in the money, ITM. The seller of the options collects the premium and keeps the stock. Another reason is to lock in substantial gains.

Example:

Juan owns several hundred shares of Dow Chemical (DOW) that he bought several years ago at $36. DOW is now selling at about $54 and he would like to lock in that gain. He chooses to sell covered calls for a $5 premium with a strike price of $49. That way, Juan becomes a writer and, unless DOW drops to or below the strike price, he collects $500 for every 100 share option he sells. And, if DOW does drop to that level before expiration, the option protects his gain of $13. (49 - 36 = 13.) per share. Good insurance.

C. Naked Calls

Naked calls occur when an investor sells a call option on a stock she does not own. Naked options are riskier than covered options and can result in almost unlimited losses. But, under the right circumstances they can be profitable. In effect, you are selling to someone else the right to buy a stock you do not own, and if required, you would have to go into the market and buy the stock at market price. This is a more advanced strategy usually limited by your broker, based on the value of your account, especially the value of the cash held in your account.

For example, Alice may choose to sell a naked call in DOW. She becomes a writer of the call. She does not own Dow shares so if the call is exercised, she would have to buy them at market and sell at the strike price. DOW is trading at about $54, so she needs to set up an out of the money option contract. Based on her reading of the market, she wants to bet that DOW will decline in price. Therefore, Alice sells a call on DOW at say, 57. That means, if the price drops below the strike price of 57, she keeps the premium and does not have to deliver the stock. If, instead, DOW surges up before the expiration date, she will have to deliver the stock. That means she must go into the market and buy DOW at the market price and deliver it. When a stock is very volatile, the potential loss can be essentially unlimited, that is, the loss is limited only by the rise in market price.

Example

Charlie has been watching Tesla Motor Company, TSLA. TSLA has recently been at about $200 but recent news causes Charlie to think the market may go down substantially. Beta for TSLA is 0.72 which means it tends to lag the market but that does not account for the recent news. Charlie sells or writes a naked call for TSLA with a strike price of $185 with a premium of $10. This means that if TSLA goes down below $185, the option will expire and he keeps the premium of $1000, that is $10 times 100 shares. His profit must be calculated with the commission included, which reduces the profit a little.

D. Credit Spreads

An option spread is another way for new traders to participate with lower risk. Unfortunately, that also means lower reward. These trades involve buying or selling two options, one at the money and one further out of the money option. For example, say Proctor and Gamble is currently at a market price of 82. An investor who owns several hundred shares of PG, structures a Bear Call Spread by selling a call on PG with a strike price of 77 for $4.75 and at the same time, buys a call at a strike price of 84 for $0.10. In this contract he collects the difference of $4.65. as long as the market stays between 77 and 84. If it stays within that range, both options will expire and he keeps the money. If PG moves above 84, he can buy the stock at 84. If PG falls below 77, which is unlikely, the option will expire.

Bull Put Spreads consist of selling a put with a strike price above current market and buying a put at an out of the money level below the current market. The gain for the investor is the difference between the two premiums, not a lot of money but low risk.

E. Butterflies and Condors

These two are low risk and low reward trades. They are based on buying and selling both puts and calls at different strike prices which bracket the market price of a stock. Gain is achieved when the stock does not move significantly by the expiration date.

Example: The Short Call Butterfly

Mary often shops at Bed, Bath and Beyond (BBBY). She knows the store is good but the common stock does not seem to be moving much at all. BBBY's beta is 0.93 which means it pretty much follows the market, so she wants to take advantage of that sideways position. BBBY has been selling at about 43, so she elects to set up a Short Call Butterfly. To do so, she sells 1 call option in the money but with a lower strike price, buys 2 call options at the money and sells 1 call option out of the money high. The following table describes her butterfly.

Action	Strike Price	Premium	Total Premium
Sell 1 Call ITM low	40	$4.00	$400
Buy 2 Calls, ATM	43	$0.92*2	-$184
Sell 1 Call OTM high	45	$0.29	$290
			Net Profit $506

Mary can collect the net premium of $506, less commissions, and pocket the profits when BBBY does not move out of that range by the expiration date. Nice profit for not doing anything.

Example: The Long Call Condor

Condors are another strategy for a sideways market but it requires four transactions, as described below, again using BBBY as our example.

The Long Call Condor

Action	Strike Price	Premium	Total Premium
Sell 1 Call ATM	43	$1.24	$124
Buy 1 Call ITM Lower	41	$0.92	- $92
Sell 1 Call OTM	43.50	$0.68	$68
Buy 1 Call OTM Higher	45	$0.19	- $19
			Net $81

This is not a high profit Condor but the is very low risk, so if Mary decides to do more than 1 contract, she can increase her profits accordingly.

There are many other combinations that we will not cover in detail here but you can learn these from your broker or at online resources.

F. Straddles and Strangles

Straddles and Strangles are more advanced trading strategies. Despite their strange sounding names, they are really rather straightforward. A straddle is a combination of a put and a call on the same underlying stock, with the same expiration date, at the current market price. Buying both a put and a call option lets you 'straddle' the stock, making a profit whether the stock goes up or down. Remember that you want to buy puts when you think the stock is going to decline in market price. You buy a call when you think the stock is going to go up in market price. When you don't know which way the stock is going to move, set up a straddle.

There are two kinds of straddles; long and short. A long straddle is one in which the investor buys the call and put options. A short straddle is one in which the investor sells both the call and the put. Notice the difference between a bull or bear spread, a butterfly or a condor in which the trader both buys and sells. In a straddle (and a strangle), the trader only buys or sells the options, but not both.

Here's an example of a straddle

Suppose Cracker Barrel Restaurants (CBRL) is currently selling at about $170 and has been for the past month. It is in a trading range of 167 to 172. Previously, it had been trading within a range of 154 to 169 for some 3 months and then made a move up. You don't know of any news that indicates it will make another move so you anticipate it will stay within its present range. This is a good time for a straddle. You could buy an ATM (at the money) call at 170 for $2.20 and a 170 put for $3.20, both with an expiration date in 2 weeks. That means you will pay $540 for the combined straddle option. Thus, if the stock moves above $172.20 you will earn a profit on the upside. If the stock declines to $166.80, you will earn a profit on the downside. In either case, the other option expires out of the money. If CBRL is still at 170 on the expiration date, you just lose the amount of the combined premiums.

Another example of a long straddle

YUM! Brands (YUM) is a collection of restaurant chains that include KFC, Pizza Hut, and Taco Bell. Recently YUM has been selling at between 82 and 85, pretty much going sideways. Mary is especially fond of YUM and thinks she can make a profit with a straddle, at a strike price of 84, so she buys a call option for $0.64 and a put for $1.65, both at a strike of 84 and the same expiration date. That means she will have an investment of $229 to construct this straddle. By the expiration date, YUM has increased to 88.20. That means she will earn money on the call option but the put will expire worthless. At $88.20, Mary has made a profit of $191, less commissions. Not bad for a two-week straddle.

On the other hand, suppose YUM had dropped to 79 by the expiration date. The call option would have expired worthless but the put option yielded $5.00 minus the combined premiums or $2.71 or $271 for the 100 shares. Again, a nice profit for a stock that is pretty much going sideways.

The other part of this strategy is the strangle. A strangle is basically the same as the straddle but uses two different strike prices, both of them OTM or out of the money. Strangles are profitable when a stock is selling within a fairly narrow trading range.

Example of a long strangle

McDonalds Corporation (MCD) has recently been trading in the range of 121 to 132. Bob wants to construct a strangle on MCD since he does not know which way the price will go but he has a suspicion it may move up. Bob buys a call with a strike price of 124, which is out of the money or OTM and a put at 117, which is also out of the money. The premium on the call is $0.04 and for the put, $0.12 for a total investment of $160. Now, if the market for MCD goes above 124, he acts on the call to make a profit and the put expires worthless. If the market drops below 117, he makes money on the put and the call expires. The total cost for this is $160, a modest bet on a market move in either direction.

CHAPTER 5 IT'S ALL GREEK TO ME

Several important features of options are measured in terms called the Greeks, and labeled with Greek letters. It is really important to understand the Greeks if you are going to get serious about trading options.

▶ **Beta**: Beta, β, is actually a characteristic of the underlying stock and measures the historical volatility of that stock. It gives equal weight to volatility on the upside as well as on the downside. When you are evaluating a stock, you can get a sense of how variable the stock's price is by looking at the β. A stable stock that moves with the market will have a beta value of about 1. If beta is less than 1, it tends to lag the market, that is a $1 movement in the market a stock with a beta less than 1 means it will increase or decrease less than $1. Conversely, a stock with a beta greater than 1 means the stock price will move more than the market, up or down. Stocks with low betas are more stable than those with a higher beta. Examples of low beta are utilities. Stocks with a high beta include industries like biotechnology.

▶ **Vega**: Vega is a measure of the volatility of the option price. The option price is related to the underlying stock price, but the option price is also variable. Vega is a measure of that volatility, but it is an implied volatility, not an historical volatility as is beta. Vega is the only Greek trading term without a Greek letter symbol.

▶ **Delta**: Delta, δ, measures the change in price of an option in response to a change in price of the underlying stock. For example, if an option has a Delta of 0.45, when the underlying stock changes by $1, the option will change by $0.45.

▶ **Gamma**: Gamma, γ, measures the rate of change in the underlying stock, not the change itself. Gamma expresses how fast the option responds to changes in Delta. Gamma is expressed as a positive or negative number. A positive gamma indicates that changes in delta will be correlated with positive movements in the underlying stock. A negative gamma has the opposite indication.

▶ **Theta**: Theta, θ, measures how much value the option will lose every day until expiration. The loss is due primarily from the time value of money. As a wasting asset, an option's value will decline because of the concept behind time value. A dollar today is worth more than a dollar next week. This time decay is difficult to calculate and most economic models are complex and often not particularly accurate.

Chapter 6 Sizing Up the Market; Predicting Directions

The world is full of uncertainty and the stock market responds accordingly. Sure, financial instruments are based on the so-called fundamentals like monetary policy, interest rates, and equity essentials like sales and taxes. We have a stereotype of market makers as being steely-eyed, cold and calculating automatons. They are not. They are human beings and are as emotionally involved in the market as any investor, 'man-on-the-street' or anyone else. Emotions often affect the market based on the sometimes irrational response to this uncertainty. Recent events like the BREXIT outcome are examples of that emotional reaction.

Basic academic economic theory assumes that investors act in a rational manner, i.e. a manner that best satisfies their own economic interests. In the real world, markets do not always act rationally because human beings do not always act rationally.

There are also certain internal events that will effect market performance like the end of quarter movements by fund managers to establish positions to make their quarterly reports look better. You can also observe drops in stock prices and indexes on Fridays, as holders get ready for the weekend by taking profits. Predicting market moves is sometimes like reading tea leaves, with a similar amount of hocus-pocus and mystery. However, successful investors learn or develop a sense of where the market is going and when. Although this book is not focused on predicting the market, all traders must have at least an intuitive feel for the market.

There are five things an investor must do in order to succeed. They are pretty obvious but we need to keep them in mind. The first is **Fundamental Analysis**. We will discuss that in this chapter in some detail. The second is **Technical Analysis,** which we will also discuss. They are sort of the 'meat and potatoes' of trading. Perhaps more important are the next three; **Intuition, Patience, and Attention**.

Intuition

Intuition can lead to many really good investments. Some years ago, a family was making regular vacation trips from Michigan to Florida. They soon noticed a new restaurant chain along the interstate highway called Cracker Barrel. Whenever they stopped at one, they had to stand in line and the food was very good and with good prices. As they made more trips, they noticed that more and more Cracker Barrel restaurants were opening, all with the same waiting line. They invested in CRBL and watched the stock rise, from their entry price of about $5.00 to today's trading range of $150 to $175. That decision was an excellent example of intuition in trading. CBRL clearly had identified a niche and filled it with good service and products.

L'eggs is a similar story. Consumers quickly reacted positively to the quality of the product and the catchy advertising, introduced in 1969. Those L'eggs plastic egg-like containers were a hit with crafts workers and carried the stock of Hanes to new highs. Many investors noticed that L'eggs was the right product at the time, was good quality and had an exciting marketing promotion. This is the essence of the Intuition component of successful investing. Look for products that are satisfying a market niche, have good quality and are well received by consumers.

Patience

Investing in the market, whether by buying and selling stocks themselves or by trading in options, requires patience. Sometimes an investor gets nervous and makes an irrational move just out of uncertainty. Traders must learn to be patient. No market moves so fast that the trader cannot make the proper trade in response to some change. Remember, options trading is not for the faint of heart. Nervous responses to extraneous conditions can wreck a well planned strategy.

Attention

There is also no substitute for paying attention to the market and your positions. No, you do not have to spend every hour of every day watching the big boards. Remember that trading options is not a 'set it and forget it' activity. Traders can build very solid portfolios and make a handsome profit, but like any other job, the trader has to be current, not just in the market moves but also in global news and reports. Some resources listed in

Chapter 7 have delightful features like daily free videos on changes in the market and outlooks from their experts. Keeping current is absolutely essential. In fact, some traders will close out all positions while they are on vacation, and then resume trading when they return. And since most people use portable computer devices; laptops, tablets, smart phones and so forth, they can spend time even on vacation, trading and investing. Either way you choose to do it, remember that options trading requires the investor to pay attention. Make that commitment before you start.

There are many tools available to traders and analysts to predict what is going to happen at least to some extent. There are two schools of thought on the subject of market predicting; technical and fundamental methods, used by informed investors. Actually, most traders use a mixture of the two.

Fundamental Analysis

Fundamental analysis looks at a number of indicators to determine, at least as an estimate, of the direction of the economy, various industry groups and individual stocks.

It begins with the general trend of the entire economy, both national and global. That old saying about the flapping wings of a butterfly in Africa causing a hurricane in Florida suggests that no national economy exists in a vacuum. There is enormous interaction between them and among them. When the general economy rises, just like the tide, all individual boats rise, but not necessarily equally. Similarly, when the economy contracts, all sectors contract but not equally. Some sectors will contract more than others. In an expanding economy, sectors like technology, biotech, electronics manufacturing, and cyclical industries like major appliances and automobiles tend to expand.

Here are some more cyclical industries:
- Heavy equipment
- Discretionary consumer goods
- Machines and tooling
- Restaurants and hotels
- Airlines

Typically, these stocks have a high Beta (β) meaning they respond quickly and strongly to fluctuations in the national and global economies.

Non-cyclical industries are those which are relatively safe during downturns, sectors like utilities, consumer staples, energy and retailers. Counter-cyclicals are those that can even thrive in economic downturns, like discount retailers, auto parts retailers and big box building suppliers.

Importantly for options traders, option prices respond to the volatility and trend of the underlying stocks so traders need to pay close attention to the economic cycle and the sectors of interest to them.

When an investor or options trader has identified the economic trend, i.e. expanding or contracting, she will then focus on a sector of interest like durable goods, finance, or hospitality, to name just a few. Within that sector or industry, she will then examine the individual companies, looking for those who will lead the way. She will do this by evaluating the company's business model, business plan, management quality and firm financials. Assessments of business models and business plans can be gained from resources like analyst's reports, annual reports and public commentary. She will examine management quality by looking at results, internal business indicators like return on investment, return on sales and debt levels compared with market capitalization. She will read and understand the various documents like the balance sheet, the income or profit and loss statement, cash flow positions and debt positions for the firm she is interested in. Most of this information is available online and through public documents including annual reports. Documents like annual reports of course, are written by insiders and may not be completely objective. Various industry analysts and experts may offer more objective insights. These are available through brokers and online sites.

Technical Analysis

Many investors base their trading decisions on technical factors which look at past performance with knowledge of present and past economic conditions. This analysis is dominated by examining charts which reflect stock performance over some period of time. Using these charts, they can estimate upcoming stock moves and therefore act on those forecasts by buying and selling options. The following charts describe some important market moves that an options trader needs to know.

The Symmetrical Triangle in Chart 1 shows a stock which is trading within a diminishing range. The upper line represents a resistance line and the lower is the support line. As the price varies between these converging lines it is often an indication of a coming breakout. With a breakout to the upside, the options trader will buy calls to cover a long position in anticipation of the upside swing. On the other hand, if the pattern shows a likelihood of a breakout below the support line, the trader might choose to buy puts in anticipation of the drop in market price.

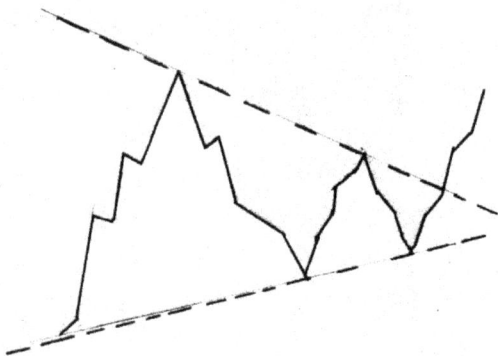

Chart 1 Triangle Pattern

Triangle patterns can also be pointed upward or downward, showing a general tendency for the stock to rise or fall.

Chart 2 shows a condition called a triple top. The horizontal dotted line below the chart is the support line and the upper dotted line is the resistance line. The chart shows the market price breaking out low. This is an occasion to sell puts. The pattern could have broken out upward, crossing the resistance line.

Notice that that chart can also be inverted, making a triple bottom. These charts indicate the direction of the stock and tips the options trader off to trade in either puts or calls.

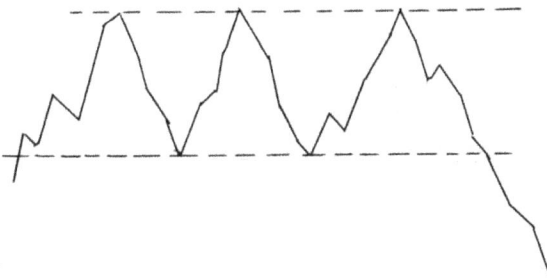

Chart 2 Triple Top

Chart 3 shows a pattern called 'head and shoulders.' This is slightly different from a triple top pattern in that the middle peak tends to be higher. Head and shoulders patterns can breakout either up or down. Either way, it presents an opportunity for options traders. The dotted line shows the recent support line. This pattern happens to break out down, but it very well could have broken out upward.

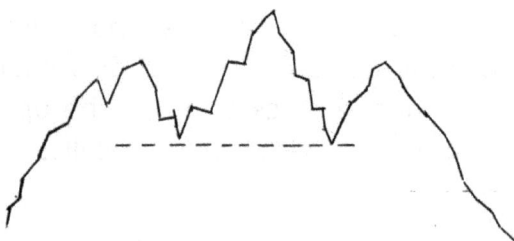

Chart 3 Head and Shoulders

Bollinger Bands

Bollinger bands are probability bands around a moving average line. These bands are usually set at either 1 or 2 standard deviations from the historic stock prices, usually the closing prices for each day. Movement outside the Bollinger Bands indicates a change in the underlying stock reflecting market changes. Breaking through the Bollinger Band acts as a signal to the options trader to take action.

There are many other technical indicators that are valuable to options traders. The various resources listed in Chapter 7 will provide excellent education and insights to both fundamental and technical analysis techniques. Most investors and traders use both fundamental and technical analysis, the combination is a personal preference. Just make sure you are familiar with the various indicators and what they can tell you. Be careful to use the correct tools for each condition. There is no "one size fits all" tool; each trader has to develop her own system of analysis. The key to success is described at the beginning of this Chapter, especially under Intuition, Patience, and Attention.

Investors of all sorts must be very careful to avoid any temptation to take action based on internal information. Option Traders and Investors can get into serious trouble if they base their investment decisions on information not available to the general public. Just don't do it is a good rule to follow. However, if you read something in the daily news or hear about it on the radio or TV, that's fine. If someone inside the company tells you some inside news not available to the general public, you may be treading on dangerous grounds. Think insider trading and Martha Stewart.

CHAPTER 7 RECOMMENDED WEBSITES AND RESOURCES FOR OPTIONS TRADING

The following are good learning resources for people starting to trade in options.

- **Simpleroptions.com** - free streamed videos and membership for access to on-line information. They have a very complete options package that will help you learn and trade and they frequently conduct live in-place and online training sessions.
- **Investopedia.com** offers extensive training through tutorials and illustrations as well as a simulator which will allow you to trade with 'virtual dollars' to learn the ropes before you go to the real market. An outstanding resource.
- **Cboe.com** - The Chicago Board of Options Exchange has both free and fee based seminars and classes as well as a virtual trading platform that allows traders to experiment and try out new strategies.

- **Technitrader.com** has an extensive series of educational videos and classes both online and in various venues.

Today, most investors trade through online brokers. It is a lot more convenient and these brokers offer all of the services and more compared with the conventional office brokers. No chasing each other on the telephone and instant access to market information and trades take place very quickly. As there are so many online brokers, we cannot tell you which is best for you, but here are a few names in no particular order. This is not an exhaustive list. We want to show you a few choices among the many available:

- tdameritrade.com has an advanced trading platform they call 'thinkorswim' with levels for 'Rookies,' 'Scholars,' and 'Gurus.' Their Education Center features good videos covering everything from introduction to options to more advanced trading strategies.
- Scottrade.com features competitive pricing and a flexible trading platform. Their Knowledge Center is

a complete resource for all kinds of trading and trades.

- Optionshouse.com offers an advanced trading platform and access to their OptionsHouse Blog with educational resources for all kinds of trading as well as tradeLAB, which offers an easy to use evaluator of risks and rewards in options trading.
- Fidelity.com advertises lower commissions and fees than several other brokers along with a full range of investor services.
- E*trade.com provides their proprietary platform at several levels called E*Trade NOW along with solid education resources including webinars and videos on a wide range of topics.
- schwab.com, part of Charles Schwab Co. offers an advanced trading platform called StreetSmart Edge with a full line of trading and research features as well as a Learning Center. They also offer workshops at their local offices to further your education.

- Tradeking.com has excellent tutoring on a variety of strategies many of which are for advanced investors. Naturally they cover all instruments; stocks, bonds, options, ETFs, Mutual Funds and more.
- Optionsxpress.com offers their Xtend trading platform and Trade and Probability Calculator that calculates probability of expiring above, below or around the strike price, giving the investor a picture of likely outcomes.
- Cboe.com is the Chicago Board of Options Exchange and has a platform based on optionsxpress.com that permits virtual trading for investors to practice and experiment with strategies. They also offer education resources at no cost and paid seminars as well as online delivery seminars.

Online Information Sources

- Yahoo Finance provides lots of information on almost all common stocks and other instruments with historic prices, options and much more.

- Google Finance provides the same kind of information as Yahoo.

Conclusion

I hope this book helped you learn the basics of options trading and the profits that can be made by engaging in this market.

The next step is to do some more research with the tools we have suggested and others you might choose. We encourage you to take advantage of the virtual platforms and practice making options trades with their digital money, not your own cash. Soon, you will feel confident enough to venture out on your own with your own broker and your own money.

If you have enjoyed this book, please be sure to leave a review and a comment to let us know how we are doing so we can continue to bring you quality books.

Thank you and good luck!

www.ingramcontent.com/pod-product-compliance
Lightning Source LLC
Chambersburg PA
CBHW050530190326
41458CB00007B/1731